The Faces of Manassas

The Faces of Manassas

Rare Photographs of Soldiers Who Fought at Bull Run

Edited by JoAnna McDonald

Rank and File Publications
1926 South Pacific Coast Highway #228
Redondo Beach, California 90277

Rank and File Publications
1926 South Pacific Coast Highway Suite 228
Redondo Beach, California 90277
(310)540-6601 books@thirdwave.net

Library of Congress Catalog Number 98-066452

ISBN Number 1-888-96701-3

Printed on recycled paper in the United States of America
Cover design by Ken Hammond

"On either side of the river there was the tree of life ...
and the leaves of the tree were for the healing of the nations."

Additional Titles Available from Rank and File Publications

A Day With Mr. Lincoln: Essays Commemorating the Lincoln Exhibition at the Huntington Library. Edited by Richard Rollins. Introduction by James McPherson. Essays by Larry Burgess, Cullom Davis, William Hanchett, John Rhodehamel and Ronald Rietveld

Blue and Gray Laughing: A Collection of Civil War Soldier's Humor
Compiled and Edited by Paul Zall

Black Southerners in Gray: Essays on Afro-Americans in Confederate Armies
Edited by Richard Rollins. Essays by Andrew Chandler Battaille, Arthur Bergeron, Thomas Cartwright, Ervin Jordan, Richard Rollins and Rudolph Young

"The Damned Red Flags of the Rebellion": The Confederate Battle Flag at Gettysburg
By Richard Rollins

"Double Canister at Ten Yards": The Federal Artillery and the Repulse of Pickett's Charge
By David Shultz

The Faces of Gettysburg: Photographs from the Gettysburg National Military Park Library
Edited by JoAnna M. McDonald

Guide to Pennsylvania Troops at Gettysburg
By Richard Rollins and David Shultz

Pickett's Charge: Eyewitness Accounts
Edited by Richard Rollins

The Returned Battle Flags **(1905)**
Edited by Richard Rollins

Table of Contents

Acknowledgments ix

Introduction x

Photographs 1

Conclusion 51

Photo Credits 52

Index by unit 54

Acknowledgments

I would like to first thank my parents, Barbara and Norman, my sisters Elizabeth and Rebecca and their families for supporting me.

One of the most influential historians in this project has been Jim Burgess, Museum Director at the Manassas National Battlefield Park. Jim provided several photographs from their archives. In addition, he directed me on a guided tour of the area.

As in my previous projects, the Military History Institute's historians, Mike Winey and Randy Hackenberg, curators, and staff at the Carlisle Barracks, Carlisle, Pennsylvania, contributed greatly and extended their cooperation above and beyond the call of duty.

In order to present to you the vast number of photographs included within, several additional archives and individuals came to my assistance: Mr. Ken Tilley of the Alabama Department of Archives and History sent me several photographs of members from the 4th Alabama, and Mr. Robert Fouts (also of Alabama) took the photos for me. Mr. John Bigham, of the South Carolina Confederate Relic Room, not only provided two photos, he also sent me information pertaining to some of the South Carolina participants. Mr. Allen Stokes and Beth Bilderback, of the South Carolina Library, University of South Carolina, Columbia, SC, provided the photo of Colonel E. B. C. Cash, 8th South Carolina. Racine County Historical Society of Racine, Wisconsin and the Milwaukee Historical Society each provided one photo of soldiers from the 2d Wisconsin. Mr. William Gladstone, Florida, also gave permission to use several of his impressive photos. Tom MacDonald, James Vickery and James Mundy, of Maine, donated many photographs to the Military History Institute where I procured the images of the 2d Maine. The Library of Congress also supplied one image. Melissa King, of ABC Photos in Manassas, helped by making negatives and copies of several photographs from the Manassas National Battlefield Park archives. Fred Pittman also copied a photograph kept by the Park. While I was unable to obtain any photographs from the Virginia Historical Society, Ms. Ann Marie F. Price was very helpful in searching their collection.

If you would like to donate an image of a soldier who fought at First Manassas (Bull Run) or Second Manassas, please contact:

Mr. James Burgess
Museum Technician
Manassas National Battlefield Park
6511 Sudley Road
Manassas, VA 20109

Lastly, I want to thank Rank and File Publications for supporting this series.

Introduction

The first large scale battle of the American Civil War is sometimes relegated to obscurity, viewed as relatively insignificant; however, to the nearly 30,000 soldiers who fought here (15,000 Union and 14,000 Confederates) this was their baptism by fire. Few warriors or politicians foresaw the carnage America would inflict upon itself in four bloody years of war, 1861-1865. This photo album includes 200 faces of those men who fought and died on the plains of Manassas Junction, Virginia, over 135 years ago.

The First Battle of Manassas (also known as Bull Run) signified the beginning of the bloodiest war in America's history. From June to July, 1861, the South concentrated an army on the southern banks of Bull Run creek near Manassas Junction, Virginia.

On Tuesday, July 16, the Union Army, commanded by Brigadier General Irvin McDowell, moved toward Manassas from Alexandria, Virginia and Washington, DC. Two days later a brigade from the Northern army was engaged in a sharp skirmish near Blackburn's Ford. Though the Union brigade was thrown back by the Confederates, the South reported 63 killed and wounded. The Union general calculated as few as 19 of his men were killed, 38 wounded, and 26 were missing.

After the fiasco at Blackburn's Ford, McDowell sent out a cavalry party and his chief engineer, John Barnard, accompanied by Governor William Sprague of Rhode Island, to find a way to turn the Confederate left flank. The group located Sudley Ford and Sudley Springs Ford several miles northwest of Blackburn's Ford, and the Union general formulated his plan.

At 2:30 a.m., July 21, two Union brigades moved out of Centreville and down the Warrenton Pike toward the stone bridge. In order to coordinate the attack, they would have to move quickly past Cub Run, allowing the main flanking force (two Union divisions, 13,000 men) to turn off the Warrenton Pike and head in a north-westerly direction toward Sudley Ford (about 8 miles away). McDowell estimated his flanking divisions would be in position by 7:00 a.m.

Finally, by 5:30 a.m., Tyler's division cleared Cub Run, and the two other divisions began their flank march toward Sudley Ford. It had taken Tyler's division (three brigades) four hours to march three miles. Between 5:15 and 6:00 a.m. his brigades deployed in the woods east of the Stone Bridge.

At 6:00 a.m., Union artillery opened fire upon Confederates deployed at the Stone Bridge about five miles southwest of Centreville, Virginia. After three hours, the battle shifted to the Matthew's Hill/Young's Branch area and continued for another three hours, until about noon, when the outnumbered Confederates retreated to Henry Hill. For an hour-and-a-half (12:00-1:30 p.m.) the Confederates organized a battle line along the southeastern edge of Henry Hill.

From 1:30-4:30 p.m. the fight raged around Henry Hill and the Chinn farm. By 4:30 p.m. the entire Union army was in full retreat. The battlefield extended over a distance of three to five miles, and within this area nearly 30,000 soldiers had participated in the conflict. General McDowell's overwhelming army had been routed.

In 10 1/2 hours, 900 men fell killed in action, another 3,000 were wounded. McDowell reported nearly 500 killed, 1,000 wounded, 1,500-1,800 missing (presumed either dead, captured, or unidentified). Most of the Union missing were captured. The Confederates counted 378 killed, 1,489 wounded and 30 missing.

Pvt. Andrew F. Ackley, age 19
Co. H, 14th Brooklyn
Survived

Capt. Alexander D. Adams, age 28
Co. B, 27th New York
Survived

Pvt. James H. Albert
Co. F, 10th Virginia
Survived

Pvt. Thomas Aldrich
Reynolds' Rhode Island Battery
Survived

Capt. Edward P. Alexander, age 26
Chief of Confederate Signal Corps
Survived

Cpl. Frederick H. Andres, age 18
Co. H, 38th New York
Survived

Capt. William Averell, USA (as Brigadier General)
Assumed command of Porter's brigade
Survived

1st Lt. Alphonso C. Avery
Co. E, 6th North Carolina
Survived

Capt. Isaac Avery, age 33
Co. E, 6th North Carolina
Wounded, Survived

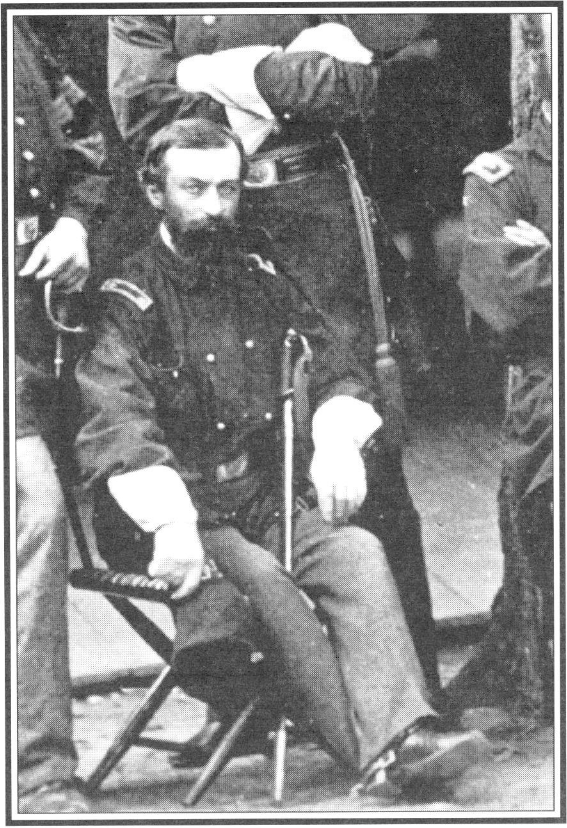

Maj. Joseph P. Balch
1st Rhode Island
Survived

Capt. Charles F. Baldwin
Co. D, 14th Brooklyn
Survived

Maj. Sullivan Ballou
2d Rhode Island
Killed

1st Lt. Charles E. Barber, age 33
Co. I, 38th New York
Survived

Adj. Theodore Barker
Hampton's South Carolina Legion
Severely wounded, Survived

Maj. John Barnard, USA
Chief of Engineers
Survived

Cpl. Alexander Barnie, Jr., age 23
Co. H, 14th Brooklyn
Survived

Pvt. John W. Barrett
Co. G, 7th Georgia
Survived

Maj. William Barry, age 43 (as a Breg. Gen.)
McDowell's Chief of Artillery
Survived

Maj. Joseph J. Bartlett, age 30
27th New York
Survived

Col. Francis Bartow, CSA
2d Brig., Johnston's Army
Killed on Henry Hill

Chaplain A. J. Bates
2d Maine
Survived

Pvt. George Baylor, age 19
Co. G, 2d Virginia
Survived

Brig. Gen. Barnard Bee, CSA
3d Brig., Johnston's Army
mortally wounded, died July 22, 1861

Cpl. John R. Bennett, age 20
Co. G, 14th Brooklyn
Survived

Col. Hiram G. Berry (as Brig. Gen.)
4th Maine
Survived

Pvt. George W. Bicknell, age 24
(as a Lieutenant)
Co. H, 5th Maine
Survived

Pvt. Sherlock F. Black
Co. C, 27th New York
Survived

Lt. William W. Blackford
1st Virginia Cavalry
Survived

Lt. Col. William Blaisdell, age 44
11th Massachusetts
Survived

Sgt. Henry N. Blake, age 22
Co. K, 11th Massachusetts
Survived

Lt. James Bloomfield
Co. E, 14th Brooklyn
Survived

Lt. Col. Joseph H. Bodin
27th New York
Survived

Pvt. John Bounds, age 18
Co. E, 27th New York
Survived

Pvt. Daniel S. Brooks, age 19
Co. A, 2d New Hampshire
Captured, died of disease Oct. '61

Pvt. Augustus T. Brown, age 22
Co. C, 14th Brooklyn
Killed

Capt. Charles C. Brown, age 33
Co. A, 13th New York
Survived

1st Lt. George T. Brown
Co. B, 2d Maine
Survived

Pvt. John C. Brown, age 20 (as Sgt.)
Co. D, 14th Brooklyn
Survived

Cpl. Francis E. Brownell
Co. A, 11th New York
Survived

Lt. Harry T. Buford
AKA: Loreta Janeta Velazquez
She wore a disguise & fought
with the Confederates -- Survived.

Pvt. Daniel E. Burbank, age 19
Co. A, 2d New Hampshire
Survived

Col. Ambrose Burnside, USA
2d Brig., Second Division
Survived

Pvt. Tzar Caldwell, age 21
Co. E, 13th New York
Survived

Col. James Cameron
7th New York
Killed

Lt. Eugene Carter, USA (as West Point Cadet)
Sykes' Regular Army Inf. Battalion
Survived

Col. E. B. C. Cash
8th South Carolina
Survived

Pvt. John Casler, age 23
Co. A, 33d Virginia
Survived

Col. John L. Chatfield
3d Connecticut
Survived

Col. George Clark, Jr.
11th Massachusetts
Survived

Capt. William Clark, Jr., age 31
Co. F, 2d Virginia
Wounded, Survived

Pvt. Henry J. Climbell
Co. C, 28th Virginia
Survived

Pvt. Jerome B. Cline
Co. D, 13th New York
Survived

Sgt. Maj. Robert T. Coles, age 19
Co. F, 4th Alabama
Survived

Capt. William Colvill, III
Co. F, 1st Minnesota
Survived

Capt. James Conner (as General)
Hampton's South Carolina Legion
Survived

Col. Michael Corcoran, age 34
69th New York Militia
Wounded, captured, Survived

Pvt. John Coxe
Hampton's South Carolina Legion
Survived

1st Lt. Lafayette Cross
Co. F, 27th New York
Survived

Pvt. James Crowell, age 30
Co. C, 4th Virginia
Killed on Henry Hill

1st Lt. George R. Davey, age 33
Co. H, 14th Brooklyn
Survived, killed at 2nd Manassas

Capt. N. H. R. Dawson
Co. C, 4th Alabama
Survived

Col. Sgt. William S. Deane, age 36
Co. A, 2d Maine
Killed

Capt. William H. DeBevoise, age 35
Co. H, 14th Brooklyn
Survived

Pvt. Joseph L. Dorrance
Co. K, 27th New York
Survived

Cpl. Thomas H. Dunham, age 22
Co. F, 11th Massachusetts
Survived

Col. John Echols
27th Virginia
Survived

1st Sgt. Charles J. Ellis
Co. K, 2d Maine
Survived

Pvt. George C. Emerson, age 23
Co. B, 2d New Hampshire
Survived

Col. Nathan Evans, CSA
7th Brig., Beaureguard's Army
Survived

Col. Noah Farnham
11th New York
Shot in the head, died Aug. 14, '61

Col. Charles Fisher
6th North Carolina
Killed

Lt. Col. Francis S. Fiske
2d New Hampshire
Survived

Sgt. Frank A. Fletcher, age 23
Co. G, 2d New Hampshire
Survived

Lt. Col. Edward B. Fowler
14th Brooklyn
Survived

Pvt. Thomas W. "Bunk" Fowler, age 27
Co. E, 5th South Carolina
Killed

Pvt. Lewis Francis, age 42
Co. I, 14th Brooklyn
Bayonetted 14 times, survived

Capt. James B. Fry, USA
A.A.G. to Gen. McDowelll
Survived

Lt. Col. William M. Gardner
8th Georgia
Wounded, survived

2d Lt. Frank A. Garnsey
Co. G, 2d Maine
Survived

Col. Lucius Gartrell
7th Georgia
Wounded, survived

Pvt. Marcelin Gauffrau, age 20
Co. H, 14th Brooklyn
Survived

Pvt. Charles G. Girardeau
Co. B, 8th Georgia
Survived

Col. William A. Gorman
1st Minnesota
Survived

Capt. Charles Griffin, age 36
Co. D, 5th U.S. Artillery
Survived

Capt. James Haggerty
Acting Lt. Col. of the 69 New York Militia
Killed

Lt. Peter Hains, age 19
Commanded the U.S. 30-pounder Parrott
Survived

2d Lt. Henry H. Seymour Hall, age 24
Co. G, 27th New York
Survived

Asst. Surg. Augustus C. Hamlin
2d Maine
Survived

Col Wade Hampton
Hampton's South Carolina Legion
Wounded, survived

Sgt. William Hanson, age 19
Co. K, 2d Maine
Killed

Pvt. Martin Haynes, age 19
Co. I, 2d New Hampshire
Survived

Cpl. Wells C. Haynes
Co. B, 2d New Hampshire
Wounded, captured, survived

Cpl. Samuel Hays, age 32
Co. E, 5th Virginia
Survived

Lt. Charles E. Hazlett, age 23
Co. D, 5th U.S. Artillery
Survived

Pvt. Harvey Holt, age 20
Co. I, 2d New Hampshire
Killed

Pvt. Charles H. Hooper
Co. B, 2d Maine
Survived

Orderly Sgt. McHenry Howard, age 22
Maryland Guard, 1st Maryland CSA
Survived

Col. O. O. Howard, USA
3d Brig. Third Division
Survived

Col. Eppa Hunton(as General)
8th Virginia
Survived

Capt. John Imboden
Staunton Artillery
Survived

Col. Charles D. Jameson
2d Maine
Survived

James Jefferson (civilian)
Fought with the 4th Alabama
Survived

Adj. John Jenkins
27th New York
Survived

Col. Micah Jenkins, age 26
5th South Carolina
Survived

Col. Egbert Jones, age 41
4th Alabama
Mortally wounded, died Sept. 3, '61

Capt. Elisha N. Jones, age 39
Co. C, 2d Maine
Killed

Pvt. Henry L. Jones, age 18
Co. G, 2d New Hampshire
Survived, died August '64

Pvt. H. S. Jones, age 19
Co. F, 14th Brooklyn
Survived

Pvt. Edwin Jordan, age 19
Co. H, 13th New York
Survived

Pvt. Edward H. Kellogg
Co. B, 38th New York
Captured, Survived

Col. Joseph Kershaw (as General)
2d South Carolina
Survived

Lt. Edmund Kirby
Co. I, 1st U.S. Artillery
Survived

Cpl. CharlesA. Knapp, age 19
Co. G, 2d Maine
Survived

Capt. Andrew Langworthy
Co. K, 2d Wisconsin
Wounded, Survived

Lt. Col. Evander Law, age 25 (as General)
4th Alabama
Wounded, Survived

Col. Samuel C. Lawrence
5th Massachusetts
Survived

Lt. William H. F. Lee
Co. E, 4th Alabama
Survived

Capt. Lewis E. Lindsay, age 41
Co. K, 4th Alabama
Killed

Pvt. Charles T. Loehr
Co. D, 1st Virginia
Survived

Pvt. Nathan N. Loud, age 23
Teamster, 1st Massachusetts
Survived

Lt. Willie P. Mangum, age 23
Co. B, 6th North Carolina
Mortally wounded, died July 29, '61

Capt. John Mansfield
Co. G, 2d Wisconsin
Survived

Col. Henry P. Martin
71st New York Militia
Survived

Col. Gilman Marston
2nd New Hampshire
Wounded, survived

Pvt. William C. Mayson
Co. B, 7th Georgia
Wounded, survived

Lt. Col. Robert McAllister, age 48
1st New Jersey
Survived

Capt. Thompson McAllister, age 50
Co. A, 27th Virginia
Survived, brother of Robert

Pvt. C. M. MeBane, age 22
Co. K, 33d Virginia
Killed

Sgt. James McKelsey
Co. K, 33d Virginia
Killed

Lt. Owen K. McLemore
CSA Artillery
Survived

Sgt. John McNeil
Co. H., 14th Brooklyn
Survived

Capt. Thomas Meagher, age 37
Co. K, 69th New York Militia
Survived

Sgt. John Merritt
Co. K, 1st Minnesota
Survived

Surg. James M. Merrow
2d New Hampshire
Survived

Orderly Sgt. William H. Morgan
Co. C, 11th Virginia
Survived

Pvt. William H. Morrill, age 18
Co. E, 2d New Hampshire
Survived, killed 1862

Surg. Samuel B. Morrison
2d Maine
Survived

1st Lt. Charles E. Mudge, age 23
Co. I, 1st Massachusetts
Survived, Killed July 3, '63

Lt. Col. Thomas Munford
30th Virginia Cavalry Battalion
Survived

Lt. Charles Norris, age 17
Co. B, 27th Virginia
Killed

Pvt. John N. Opie, age 17
Co. L, 5th Virginia
Survived

Pvt. Edward F. Orff, Jr., age 20
Co. G, 2d Maine
Killed

Pvt. William B. Ott, age 21
Co. I, 4th Virginia
Killed

Cpl. William L. Paxton, age 22
Co. I, 4th Virginia
Killed

Lt. John Pelham, CSA
Wise Artillery
Survived

Col. Isaac F. Quimby
13th New York
Survived

Lt. Doug Ramsay
Co. I, 1st U.S. Artillery
Killed

Capt. Charles E. Rand, age 28
Co. I, 1st Massachusetts
Survived, killed in '63

2d Lt. N. W. Ray, age 21
Co. D, 6th North Carolina
Survived

Capt. William H. Reynolds
Captain of a Rhode Island Battery
Survived

Pvt. Elisha H. Rhodes (as Colonel)
Co. D, 2d Rhode Island
Survived

Pvt. John L. Rice, age 21
Co. A, 2d New Hampshire
Wounded and captured

Capt. James B. Ricketts, age 44 (as Brigadier General)
Co. I, 1st U.S. Artillery
Wounded, captured, Survived

Capt. Hiram Rollins, age 34
Co. D, 2d New Hampshire
Severely wounded, survived

Lt. Charles C. Sale
Co. I, 4th Alabama
Survived

Sgt. Charles Schurig, age 25 (as Lieutenant)
Co. H, 14th Brooklyn
Survived

Pvt. James E. Saunders, age 30 (as Captain)
Co. G, 2d New Hampshire
Survived

Pvt. Lawrence H. Scruggs
Co. I, 4th Alabama
Survived

Col. William T. Sherman, USA
3d Brig., First Division
Survived

Col. Henry W. Slocum
27th New York
Wounded, survived

Col. John Slocum
2d Rhode Island
Killed

Lt. Benjamin R. Smith, age 20
Co. G, 6th North Carolina
Survived

Capt. S. James Smith
Co. I, 2d Rhode Island
Killed

Col. William Smith, age 65
49th Virginia Battalion
Survived

Lt. William H. B. Smith, age 38
Co. G, 1st Massachusetts
Killed, July 18, '61

1st Lt. Horatio Staples
Co. G, 2d Maine
Survived

Lt. Col. Carl Stephan
13th New York
Survived

Pvt. Daniel D. Stillwell
Co. B, 13th New York
Survived

Capt. Ebenezer W. Stone, age 23
Co. D, 1st Massachusetts
Survived

Capt. Jeremiah A. Sullivan
Co. B, 13th New York
Survived

1st Lt. William H. Swan, age 44
Co. B, 27th New York
Survived

Maj. George Sykes (seen as Maj. Gen.)
U.S. Regular Infantry Battalion
Survived

Capt. Samuel M. Tate, age 30 (as a Colonel.)
Co. D, 6th North Carolina
Survived

Pvt. James S. Thomas, age 19
Co. D, 11th Massachusetts
Survived

Capt. Levi Tower
Co. F, 2d Rhode Island
Killed

Cpl. W. G. Turner, age 24
Co. E, 6th North Carolina
Survived

Cpl. Willie Upham
Co. F, 2d Wisconsin
Wounded, Survived

Maj. George Varney
2d Maine
Survived

Dr. Watkins Vaughan (civilian)
Fought with the 4th Alabama

Maj. James Wadsworth (as Brigadier General)
Led the 2d Wisconsin into battle
Survived

Quartermaster-Sgt. Fergus Walker, age 26
Co. K, 38th New York
Survived

Col. Hobart J. Ward, age 38
38th New York
Survived

Maj. R. F. Webb, age 38
6th North Carolina
Survived

Pvt. Daniel Webster, age 21
Co. G, 27th New York
Survived, died of disease, 1862

Lt. William Weeden
Reynolds' Rhode Island Battery
Survived

Pvt. Nemiah Westbrook, age 28
Co. G, 27th New York
Survived

Maj. C. R. Wheat
Wheat's Louisiana Inf. Battalion
Wounded, Survived

Lt. Col. Frank Wheaton
2d Rhode Island
Survived

Sgt. Henry C. Wheeler, age 21
Co. C, 27th New York
Survived

Lt. B. F. White
Co. F, 6th North Carolina
Survived

Pvt. Benjamine S. White, age 19
Co. G, 2d Virginia
Survived

Col. Henry Whiting
2d Vermont
Survived

1st Lt. John H. Whitten
Co. A, 11th Massachusetts
Survived

1st Lt. John M. Wilson (left)
2d U.S. Artillery
Survived

Col. Alfred M. Wood
14th Brooklyn
Wounded, Survived

Chaplain Augustus Woodbury
1st Rhode Island
Survived

Capt. Daniel Woodbury
Corp. of Engineers, U.S.A.
Survived

Pvt. William Woodward, age 30
Co. L, 5th Virginia
Killed

Capt. William B. Yancey
Co. E, 10th Virginia
Survived

Lt. James H. Young, age 36
Co. K, 4th Alabama
Survived

Conclusion

Word of the encounter at Manassas brought a shocked response throughout America and the world. Enlisted men and officers had faced the trauma of warfare: they had witnessed the death of their friends and raised their hands against fellow Americans. Clearly, as had been predicted by the regular officers, the volunteers needed more discipline, drilling, and better equipment as they faced an escalation of hostility.

Though some enthusiastic Confederates wished to pursue the Union Army and capture the Capitol, Private Berrien Zettler, 8th Georgia, hoped the fighting was over. While walking among the dead he reasoned: "'Surely, surely, there will never be another battle.' It seemed . . . barbarous for men to try to settle any dispute or controversy by shooting one another, and, now that it had been realized what a battle meant, I felt sure there would never be another."

Many of the Union soldiers felt as Zettler. They had experienced enough fighting; the three-month enlistments were up and some of the men returned home. The soldiers who remained rested, drilled, and combated camp diseases.

Newspapers reacted strongly to the events of July 21. The *Richmond Whig* arrogantly proclaimed: "The breakdown of the Yankee race, their unfitness for empire, forces dominion on the South. We are compelled to take the sceptre of power. We must adapt ourselves to our new destiny. We must elevate our race, every man of it, breed them up to arms, to command, to empire."

In the North naive thoughts of a quick victory and a reasonably bloodless war were shattered. Shock and dismay spread throughout the population when they heard the tragic news; their powerful Northern army had been humiliated. Yet, once the initial surprise had passed, the North reacted with vengeful enthusiasm.

Europe watched in curious dismay. Observing America's reaction, the London Daily News predicted, "The grand controversy between the North and the South has at length reached the point it has been for years past gradually approaching -- the ultimate ratio of force; and the sword having now been drawn in earnest, it must be fought out."

Appendix
States Represented at First Manassas and their Killed and wounded

Confederates

Alabama: 40 Killed; 156 wounded
Georgia: 60 Killed; 293 wounded
Louisiana: 11 Killed; 58 wounded
Maryland: 1 Killed; 5 wounded
Mississippi: 43 Killed; 147 wounded
North Carolina: 24 Killed; 53 wounded
South Carolina: 44 Killed; 268 wounded
Tennessee: 1 Killed; 3 wounded
Virginia: 174 Killed; 579 wounded*

Union

Connecticut: 6 Killed; 26 wounded
Maine: 57 Killed; 118 wounded
Massachusetts: 14 Killed; 67 wounded
Michigan: 6 Killed; 37 wounded
Minnesota: 42 Killed; 108 wounded
New Hampshire: 9 Killed; 35 wounded
New Jersey: rear-guard -- no casualties
New York: 236 Killed; 449 wounded**
Ohio: 2 Killed; 6 wounded
Rhode Island: 38 Killed; 102 wounded
Vermont: 6 Killed; 22 wounded
Wisconsin: 24 Killed; 65 wounded

U.S. Artillery: 22 Killed; 39 wounded
U.S. Cavalry: 13 wounded
U.S. Infantry: 10 Killed; 20 wounded
U.S. Marines: 9 Killed; 19 wounded

*Suffered the highest casualties of any state -- 753.
**Second highest casualties of any state -- 685.

Photo Credits

Histories = *Histories of the Several Regiments and Battalions from North Carolina in the Great War 1861-1865*, 1901.

Millers's = Miller's Photograhic History of the Civil War

MNP = Manassas National Battlefield Park

Second New Hampshire = *A History of the Second Regiment, New Hampshire Volunteer Infantry*, 1896.

USAMHI = United States Military History Institute, Carlisle, Pennsylvania

Pvt. Andrew F. Ackley, USAMHI

Capt. Alexander D. Adams, Roger Hunt Collection via USAMHI

Pvt. James H. Albert, Ronald L. Harris Collection via USAMHI

Pvt. Thomas Aldrich. *The History of Battery A, First Rhode Island Light Artillery in the War to Preserve the Union 1861-1865*, 1904.

Capt. Edward P. Alexander, USAMHI

Cpl. Frederick H. Andres, USAMHI

Capt. William Averell, USAMHI

1st Lt. Alphonso C. Avery. *Histories*

Capt. Isaac Avery, *Histories*

Maj. Joseph P. Balch, USAMHI

Capt. Charles F. Baldwin, USAMHI

Maj. Sullivan Ballou, USAMHI

Adj. Theodore Barker, Dr. Gaillard Waterfall Collection via South Carolina Confederate Relic Room and Museum, Columbia, SC

Maj. John Barnard, USAMHI

Cpl. Alexander Barnie, Jr., USAMHI

Pvt. John W. Barrett, MNP

Maj. Joseph J. Bartlett, Roger Hunt Collection via USAMHI

Col. Francis Bartow, USAMHI

Chaplain A. J. Bates, USAMHI

Pvt. George Baylor, Dickinson College Spahr Library

Brig. Gen. Barnard Bee, USAMHI

Cpl. John R. Bennett, Shelby Co. Historical Society via USAMHI

Col. Hiram Berry, USAMHI

Pvt. George W. Bicknell, USAMHI

Pvt. Sherlock F. Black, USAMHI

Lt. William W. Blackford. *War Years with Jeb Stuart* (New York: Charles Scribner's Sons) 1945.

Lt. Col. William Blaisdell, USAMHI

Sgt. Henry N. Blake, USAMHI

Lt. James Bloomfield, USAMHI

Lt. Col. Joseph H. Bodin, USAMHI

Pvt. John Bounds, USAMHI

Pvt. Daniel S. Brooks. *Second New Hampshire*

Pvt. Augustus T. Brown, USAMHI

Capt. Charles C. Brown, USAMHI

1st Lt. George I. Brown, Tom MacDonald via James Mundy via USAMHI

Pvt. John C. Brown, Tom Clemens Collection via USAMHI

Cpl. Francis E. Brownell, USAMHI

Lt. Harry T. Buford. *The Woman in Battle,* 1876.

Pvt. Daniel E. Burbank. *Second New Hampshire*

Col. Ambrose Burnside, Klinepeter Collection via USAMHI

Pvt. Tzar Caldwell, USAMHI

Col. James Cameron, USAMHI

Lt. Eugene Carter, USAMHI

Col. E. B. C. Cash, South Caroliniana Library, Univ. of South Carolina, Columbia, SC

Pvt. John Casler. *Four Years in the Stonewall Brigade*

Col. John L. Chatfield, USAMHI

Col. George Clark, Jr., USAMHI

Capt. William Clark, Jr., Herren Collection via USAMHI

Pvt. Henry J. Climbell, Ardis J. Rahe Collection via USAMHI

Pvt. Jerome B. Cline, USAMHI

Sgt. Maj. R. T. Coles, Alabama Department of Archives and History, Montgomery, Alabama.

Capt. William Colvill, III, USAMHI

Capt. James Conner, Millers vol. 10

Col. Michael Corcoran, USAMHI

Pvt. John Coxe, Confederate Veteran, Vol. 23 (1915)

1st Lt. Lafayette Cross, Loretta Avery Collection via USAMHI

Pvt. James Crowell, Crowell Collection via USAMHI

1st Lt. George R. Davey, USAMHI

Capt. N. H. R. Dawson, Alabama Department of Archives and History

Color-Sgt. William S. Deane, James Vickery Collection via USAMHI

Capt. William H. DeBevoise, USA MHI

Pvt. Joseph L. Dorrance, Donald Wisoski Collection via USAMHI

Cpl. Thomas H. Dunham, Roger Hunt Collection via USAMHI

Col. John Echols, USAMHI

1st Sgt. Charles J. Ellis, Tom MacDonald via James Mundy via USAMHI

Pvt. George C. Emerson, *Second New Hampshire*

Col. Nathan Evans, USAMHI

Col. Noah Farnham, USAMHI

Col. Charles Fisher. *Second New Hampshire*

Lt. Col. Edward B. Fowler, USAMHI

Pvt. Thomas W. Fowler, Union County Museum via South Carolina Confederate Relic room and Museum

Pvt. Lewis Francis. *The Medical and Surgical History of the War of the Rebellion*, Part 3, Vol. 2, 1883.

Capt. James B. Fry, USAMHI

Lt. Col. William M. Gardner, Miller, Vol. 10

2d Lt. Frank A. Garnsey, James Vickery via James Mundy via USAMHI

Col. Lucius Gartrell, Miller, Vol. 10

Pvt. Marcelin Gauffrau, USAMHI

Pvt. Charles G. Girardeau, Robert G. Carroon Collection via USAMHI

Col. William Gorman, USAMHI

Capt. Charles Griffin, USAMHI

Capt. James Haggerty, USAMHI

Lt. Peter Hains, USAMHI

2d Lt. Henry H. Seymour Hall, USAMHI

Asst. Surg. Augustus C. Hamlin, USAMHI

Col. Wade Hampton, USAMHI

Sgt. William Hanson, Tom MacDonald Collection via James Mundy via USAMHI

Pvt. Martin Haynes. *Second New Hampshire*

Cpl. Wells C. Haynes. *Second New Hampshire*

Cpl. Samuel Hays, Edward Franks Collection via USAMHI

Lt. Charles E. Hazlett, USAMHI

Pvt. Harvey Holt. *Second New Hampshire*

Pvt. Charles H. Hooper, Tom MacDonald Collection via James Mundy via USAMHI

Orderly Sgt. William H. Morgan. *Personal Reminiscences of the War of 1861-1865* (Lynchburg: J. P. Bell Co.) 1911.

Col. O. O. Howard, USAMHI

Col. Eppa Hunton, Miller, Vol. 10

Capt. John Imboden, USAMHI

Col. Charles D. Jameson, USAMHI

James Jefferson. *Reuben Vaughan Kidd: Soldier of the Confederacy* (Petersburg: Violent Bank), 1947.

Adj. John Jenkin, William Gladstone Collection via USAMHI

Col. Micah Jenkins, Miller Vol. 10

Col. Egbert Jones, Alabama Department of Archives and History, Montgomery, Alabama

Capt. Elisha N. Jones, Tom MacDonald via James Mundy via USAMHI

Pvt. Henry L. Jones, *Second New Hampshire*

Pvt. Edwin Jordan, USAMHI

Pvt. Edward H. Kellogg, USAMHI

Col. Joseph Kershaw, USAMHI

Lt. Edmund Kirby, USAMHI

Cpl. Charles A. Knapp, Tom MacDonald via James Mundy via USAMHI

Capt. Andrew Langworthy, Milwaukee Historical Society

Lt. Col. Evander Law, USAMHI

Col. Samuel C. Lawrence, USAMHI

Lt. William H. F. Lee, Alabama

Capt. Lewis E. Lindsay, Quinn Collection via USAMHI

Pvt. T. Loehr, USAMHI

Pvt. Nathan N. Loud, USAMHI

Lt. Willie Mangum. *Histories,* Vol. 1

Capt. John Mansfied, Library of Congress, LCB 812

Col. Henry P. Martin, USAMHI

Col. Gilman Marston, USAMHI

Pvt. William C. Mayson, USAMHI

Lt. Col. Robert McAllister, USAMHI

Capt. Thompson McAllister. *Sketch of Captain Thompson McAllister, Citizen, Soldier,* Christian, 1896.

Sgt. James McKelsey, MNP

Lt. Owen K. McLemore, Alabama Department of Archives and History

Sg.t. John McNeil, USAMHI

Pvt. C. M. Mebane, *Histories* Vol. 1

Sgt. John Merritt, USAMHI

Sgt. James M. Merrow, *Second New Hampshire*

Orderly-Sgt. William H. Morgan. *Personal Reminiscences of the War of 1861-1865* (Lynchburg: J. P. Bell Co.) 1901.

Pvt. William H. Morrill. *Second New Hampshire*

Surg. Samuel B. Morrison, James Mundy via USAMHI

1st Lt. Charles E. Mudge, USAMHI

Lt. Col. Thomas Munford, USAMHI

Lt. Charles Norris, MNP

Pvt. John N. Opie. *A Rebel Cavalryman with Lee, Stuart and Jackson*, 1899

Pvt. Edward F. Orff, James Vickery Collection via James Mundy via USAMHI

Pvt. William Ott, MNP

Cpl. William Paxton, MNP

Lt. John Pelham, USAMHI

Col. Isaac F. Quinby, USAMHI

Capt. Charles E. Rand, USAMHI

Lt. Doug Ramsay, Borrell, Sr., Collection via USAMHI

2d Lt. N. W. Ray. *Histories*

Capt. William H. Reynolds. *The History of Battery A ...*, 1904.

Pvt. Elisha H. Rhodes, USAMHI

Pvt. John L. Rice. *Second New Hampshire*

Capt. James B. Ricketts, USAMHI

Capt. Hiram Rollins. *Second New Hampshire*

Lt. Charles C. Sale, Alabama Department of Archives and History, Montgomery, Alabama

Pvt. James E. Saunders. *Second New Hampshire*

Sgt. Charles Schurig, USAMHI

Pvt. Lawrence H. Scruggs, Alabama Department of Archives

Col. William T. Sherman, USAMHI

Col. Henry W. Slocum. *Histories of the 27th Regiment New York Volunteers*, 1888

Col. John Slocum, USAMHI

Lt. Benjamin R. Smith. *Histories*

Capt. S. James Smith, William Gladstone Collectin via USAMHI

Col. William Smith, USAMHI

Lt. William H. B. Smith, USAMHI

Lt. Col. Carl Stephan, USAMHI

Pvt. Daniel D. Stillwell, Chris Jordan Collection via USAMHI

Capt. Ebenezer W. Stone, USAMHI

Capt. Jeremiah A. Sullivan, USAMHI

1st Lt. William H. Swan, USAMHI

Maj. George Sykes, USAMHI

Capt. Samuel M. Tate. *Histories*

Pvt. James S. Thomas, USAMHI

Capt. Levi Tower, USAMHI

Cpl. W. G. Turner. *Histories*

Cpl. Willie Upham, Racine County Militant (1915) via Racine Heritage Museum, Racine, Wisconsin

Maj. George Varney, Tom MacDonald Collection via James Mundy via USAMHI

Dr. Watkin Vaughan. *Reuben Vaughan Kidd: Soldier of the Confederacy* (Petersburg: Violent Bank), 1947

Maj. James Wadsworth, USAMHI

Quartermaster-Sgt. Fergus Walker, William Styple Collection via USAMHI

Col. Hobart J. Ward, USAMHI

Pvt. Daniel Webster, USAMHI

Lt. William Weeden. *History of Battery A ...*

Pvt. Nemiah Westbrook, USAMHI

Maj. C. R. Wheat. *Confederate Veteran*, vol. 19

Lt. Col. Frank Wheaton, USAMHI

Sgt. Henry C. Wheeler, USAMHI

Lt. B. F. White. *Histories*

Pvt. Benjamin S. White, Ed Luhn Collection via USAMHI

Col. Henry Whiting, USAMHI

1st Lt. John H. Whitten, USAMHI

1st Lt. John Wilson, USAMHI

Col. A. M. Wood, USAMHI

Chap. Augustus Woodbury, USAMHI

Capt. Daniel P. Woodbury, USAMHI

Pvt. William Woodward. *A Rebel Cavalryman with Lee, Stuart and Jackson*, 1899

Capt. William B. Yancey, USAMHI

Lt. James H. Young, Alabama Department of Archives and History, Montgomery, Alabama

Federal Index

Artillery: 1, 5, 21, 22, 24, 28, 38, 39, 47, 49
Brigadiers: 2, 11, 5
Brooklyn, 14th: 1, 3, 4, 6, 8, 9, 10, 15, 16, 19(2), 21, 27, 33, 39, 49
Connecticut:, 3rd: 12
Engineers: 4, 8, 50
Massachusetts:
 1st: 30, 3, 37, 42, 43
 5th: 29
 11th: 13, 17, 44, 49
Maine:
 2nd: 6, 10, 16, 17, 20, 22, 23, 24, 26, 27, 29, 35, 36, 42, 45
 4th: 7
 5th: 7

Minnesota, 1st: 14, 21, 34
Miscellaneous: 20, 40
New Hampshire, 2nd: 9, 11, 17, 18, 19, 23(2), 24, 27, 31, 34(2), 38, 39, 40
New Jersey, 1st: 32
New York:
 7th: 11
 11th: 10, 18
 13th: 9, 11, 13, 28, 37, 42(2), 43
 27th: 1, 5, 7, 9, 15, 16, 22, 26, 40, 43, 46, 47, 48
 38th: 2, 4, 8, 28, 46(2)
 69th: 14, 22, 33
 71st: 31
Rhode Island:
 1st: 3, 49
 2nd: 3, 38, 41(2), 44, 47
 Artillery: 38, 47
U.S. Regulars: 12, 24, 37, 43, 49
Vermont, 2nd: 48
Wisconsin, 2nd: 29, 31, 45(2)

Confederate Index

Alabama, 4th: 14, 16, 25, 26, 27, 29, 30(2), 39, 40, 45, 50
Artillery: 25, 33, 37
Brigadiers: 5, 6
Georgia:
 7th: 5, 20, 32
 8th: 20
Louisiana, Wheat's Battalion:
Maryland, 1st Cavalry: 25
North Carolina, 6th: 2, 3, 18, 31, 38, 41, 44(2), 46, 48
Signal Corps: 2
South Carolina:
 2nd: 28
 5th: 18, 26
 8th: 12, 21
 Hampton's Legion: 4, 8, 14, 15, 23
Virginia:
 1st: 30
 2nd: 6, 13, 48
 4th: 15, 36(2)
 5th: 24, 36, 50
 7th: 33
 8th: 25
 10th: 1, 50
 11th: 34
 27th: 17, 32, 35
 28th: 13
 33rd: 12, 32, 33
 49th Btn: 41
 1st Cavalry: 7
 30th Cavalry Btn: 35